THE
LOST
CHILD
Of
WWII

My Life during the Great War

LEONIDA CLARETE-WATSON

The Lost Child of WWII
Copyright © 2020 by Leonida Clarete-Watson

Library of Congress Control Number: 2020912251
ISBN-13: Hardcover: 978-1-64749-173-4
          Epub: 978-1-64749-174-1

Printed in the United States of America

 GoTo Publish

GoToPublish LLC
1-888-337-1724
www.gotopublish.com
info@gotopublish.com

Contents

Volume I

Chapter 1

I love family reunions. I look forward to them every year. I think it's because I love being surrounded by family the laughter and chaos that only the closeness of a family can produce. Filling the house with echoes of my children, and now with my children's children, as they energetically scamper from room to room producing piercing screams and laughter as they play. My heart fills with happiness and delight as I sit back and watch silently, soaking in the blessings God has bestowed on me.

But at night, as I sit at my dining room table drinking my hot tea and when all the little ones are down in a deep sleep, exhausted from the long day of play, and the house becomes still and quiet, my mind takes me back to the horrible days of my past. I try to shake the feeling and desperately try to focus on what I have today. My lovely home, my family, and my loving husband—but it's part of me, and it has made me the strong, confident woman I am today. I ultimately give in and relive the pain of my own childhood.

My name is Leonida. but people just call me Nida. I grew up in the Philippines during the great war of my time. I had a loving father who adored me. He was my protector and teacher. He was my rock, my hero, my father. He made me feel safe and he shaped me into the person I am today. Without his love and teachings of what is right, I strongly believe that I wouldn't have what I have today. I may be overstating him a bit: my last memory of him was when I was only four years old, yet even at that young of an age, he captivated my imagination with his stories. I remember walking with him when I was even younger. I guess my earliest memory was from when I was as young as two years old. He was my inspiration and my hope, and he was taken from me when I was just four years old. I watched with tears in my eyes as he was killed at the hands of the Japanese for safeguarding some Americans by hiding them in a cave. I will never forget his last words to me. "Be strong, Nida, I love you."

I often wonder what my life would have been like if my father had been around. But since he was no longer around, he left me with his lessons that I have carried with me and that gave me the inner strength it would take to survive. I did the best I could with what I had and with every opportunity that came my way, even when I was sold to another family so my mother could buy medicine.

But I'm getting ahead of myself. Let me take you back to the earliest childhood memory I have of my father. Growing up in the province of Pampanga, just outside the city of Porac, we didn't have a lot of money. We lived in a small hut in a small village just south of the province. Like many families back then, we made do with what we had and struggled just to get by like everyone else at that time. My father was in the Philippine Army, and he would be gone for weeks at a time, sometimes months at a time. But I always knew when he returned home because I would awake to a bunch of grapes on my pillow. I would smile as I awoke and whisper, "Daddy's home."

I had several brothers and sisters, but I was the baby and the only one who really captured my father's affection. Every time he would come home, I would see the grapes on my pillow, and I would be the only one to get them. I learned to share with my siblings rather quickly at such a young age, which dissipated any envy and helped make my brothers and sisters look after me. I guess I was two years old when my father started leaving grapes on my pillow.

It was so nice to have my father home since he was away so much. We would take walks out along the dirt road of my village, and everyone would wave and yell "welcome home" to him as we walked. Some would even stop what they were doing in the rice paddies or fields just to come up and say hello to us.

He would often tell me stories about his time away with his troops and the training they had gone through that month, but I didn't understand a lot of it back then and just looked up at him with a big smile across my face as we walked hand in hand down the road toward the market.

I remember he would always ask me, "What would you do?" during our conversations about trivial matters. To him, it was important, so I would think hard and come up with a story on how I would deal with the subject at hand. He would listen to me intently as I would tell him how I would tell the person who said something bad about me that it wasn't a very nice thing to say, especially when what he said was wrong, and next time he should just ask me and I would tell him what the truth was. He would say, "That's very good, Nida, you're a smart little girl."

Once we arrived at the market, my dad would haggle with the vendors until he walked away and they would yell at him to come back and he could pay the price he originally suggested. Sometimes he would go back and buy the item, but other times, as he walked away, he would say, "You had your chance. I will get it somewhere else.'

I do remember this one time in particular that he walked away. The vendor followed him and kept lowering his price until my father turned and said, "Fine, I will take all you have." The biggest smile you would have ever seen crossed the vendor's face as he raced back to grab his merchandise for my father. I guess you could say he loved to haggle.

But even with our trip to the markets, a lesson was to be learned. He would tell me, "Don't let anyone ever sell you on something that you don't really want or need, and never buy something just because you can."

Chapter 2

A few months later. the Japanese invaded the Philippine islands and made their way toward my village in a matter of a few days. My father had already left to go back to his unit a few weeks before the Japanese came and was gone until the day before they arrived at my village. It was a scary time for everyone. The Japanese would kill people indiscriminately for hiding when they arrived or even entire families for coming out with their hands in the air. Some people they would leave alone as they made their way to my village while slaughtering others for reasons only they understood.

Like I said, my father returned home the day before the Japanese arrived at my village, but something was wrong. I awoke to the sound of his voice. but when I looked on my pillow, there were no grapes. My brothers and sisters were already awake and out in the main living area as I walked out.

My father was talking to my brothers and holding each one by their shoulders as he faced them. They would nod their heads and say yes or okay. and then my father would hug them and move to the next in line.

I walked out into the living area, and my mother was crying. I started to make my way over to her. but my father stepped in front of me and told me to get dressed. I looked at my mom, and she didn't look back at me. So, I went and got dressed. I barely had time to put my sandals on when my brother David came in to get me.

"Come on. Nida- we're going with Dad, and we have to leave now," he said.

As my brother took my hand and led me out of the room. I could see that my father had changed out of his uniform and put on his backpack. which looked completely filled with stuff. My father took me and my brother out of the village, and we walked for hours at a rather quick pace. I had to run a lot to keep up. After what seemed to be an eternity on the dirt roads and paths, we took a turn and made our way through the forested area. After another long while, we finally broke through the trees and made our way to the mountainside where there was a cave opening.

My father told us to wait and for my brother to keep alert. My brother and I waited outside the opening as my father made his way inside. I watched intently as my father entered the opening, and I could see a few white people in uniform meet him partially in the cave before they disappeared into the dark hole.

My brother was walking in a large semicircle behind me, looking out at the trees as he slowly paced back and forth. I had never seen him so serious before, and I started to get a little scared. But he told me, "Not now, Nida. Be strong and wait for Dad to come back," as his eyes continued to scan through the trees and never once looked over at me while he spoke.

My father was in there for a little while before he emerged from the cave and headed toward us. He didn't have his backpack anymore and was walking at an even quicker pace than on the way out here.

As we headed back through the forest trees, I asked my father, "Who are those men?"

He replied. "American soldiers."

"Why are they in the cave?" I asked.

"I'm hiding them from the Japanese," he said without turning around, continuing through the trees.

"Why do they have to hide from the Japanese?"

My father stopped and looked back at me. He got down on one knee and said, "Because, Nida, we are at war, and the Japanese are the enemy of Filipino. But the Americans are our friends. And the

Japanese are killing all Americans they come across. So, I 'm hiding them to keep them alive."

He grabbed my shoulders like I had seen him do to my brothers and looked me right in the eyes and said, "I need you to be strong. Nida, and I know you can be. Can you be strong for me?"

I looked into my father's brown eyes and had never seen his eyes look at me so intently before. I was really scared, but I wanted to be brave for my father. So, I nodded my head.

He gave me a hug and said, "That's my girl. Now we had better get back to the village."

We walked just as quickly on the way back as we did coming out to the cave. The morning had passed long ago and was well into the late afternoon when we made our way to our village. Some people in the village were packing their belongings into carts or big bags and carrying them away as we walked toward our house. It's strange, but even at the age of only three years old. I knew why they were leaving. They were scared and were fleeing for their lives because the Japanese were on their way.

My father would talk to a few of our neighbors, but only briefly, before saying goodbye to them and we would continue toward our hut.

I will never forget the panic I saw on the faces of my fleeing neighbors of the village. It was the first time I had seen fear. I would look at my father's face and see only determination. It's strange, but I knew I didn't want to look how my neighbors looked, so I pinched my lips together like my father and slightly squinted my eyes. I was brave on the inside, so I wanted to show I was brave on the outside.

When we got home, we found that my family had been busy gathering food and other supplies inside the living area of our home.

We spent the rest of the day organizing and hiding some of the supplies. Some of the neighbors who were staying came by to speak

with my father throughout the day. I don't know for sure about what, but I guessed it had something to do with the men he was hiding because I heard one of them yell, "You're putting your family and the rest of us at risk for those Americans!" My father quickly stood toe-to-toe with him and said something that I couldn't hear.

The man backed up and put up his hands before turning around and leaving. As my father turned, he noticed I had witnessed the disagreement and gave me a wink and a smile. After I smiled back, he quickly put on his stern face and went back to work.

That evening, we all sat in the living area and had a big meal of pork, cabbage, and rice. We all ate our fill and went to our bedrolls.

The next morning, I awoke to screams coming from the village. I looked around. My brothers and sisters jumped to their feet, so I did too.

We ran out to the living area and could see my father at the door. He told all of us to come with him, so we followed him through the village to the tree line where he had us hide.

The earth was wet from the storm last night, and I started to get chilled because I was still in my nightclothes. My older sister Shanida removed her scarf and wrapped it around my neck and shoulders.

We all hid at the edge of our village as the Japanese came through. Shots would ring out and screaming came from the village for what seemed to be hours, but I don't think it was, because the sun had still not come close to reaching the top of the sky.

My father came up to me and picked me up. He told the rest of the kids to stay hidden. Then he said something to my mother, and they started walking toward the road that led to our village. I started to get tears in my eyes, and my father said, "Be brave, Nida, and everything will be okay."

We walked up to the village, and we were immediately stopped by a couple of Japanese soldiers. My father held me tight, which was really comforting, but I was still really scared. The Japanese soldiers were yelling and pointing their guns at us. My mother started to cry, and my father got down on his knees, refusing to let me go. Another Japanese soldier yelled something, and my father shook his head no.

"I'm a farmer. The rest of my kids are out in the paddy fields," he said.

The soldiers talked among one another for a bit. Then a soldier farther into the village yelled something, and two of the soldiers that were with us ran toward him. The remaining soldier asked my father something, and my father pointed to our hut. He motioned with his gun for us to go there and walked off toward his comrades.

Chapter 3

The Japanese had taken over our village in less than a half hour and had been patrolling through our village over the last three weeks. My father had managed to convince them that he was a simple farmer, and they had spared our lives that day. But my father still had a sense of duty to those trying to help us from the invading forces, and it became a sense of pride for me to know my father was willing to sacrifice his life to help the Americans.

Although a tremendous burden lay on my father's shoulders, he did not carry it alone. My brothers and I would help him keep the American GIs safe. Feeding them what we could find and scavenge from the locals.

I was often called on to go through Japanese fire to fetch potatoes for the Americans. I guess it was because I was the smallest.

"Okay. Nida- you stay on your belly and scoot yourself across the field. Keep your head down close to the ground, and the Japanese won't be able to see you," Father said as he demonstrated a low-crawl maneuver, using his arms and legs in a snakelike fashion to propel himself across the ground.

I admit that the first time I crawled out into the open grassy field I was scared. But I started out into the field because I trusted my father and I knew that the Americans we had hidden in the caves earlier were very hungry.

I could hear the bullets fly overhead with a twirling sound of air almost like a whizzing noise. I made it to the potatoes and put a few in my bag that was wrapped around my neck and shoulder before heading back. I kept my face to the ground as I wiggled my way toward my father and brothers, who were waiting for me along the tree line. I was only about ten feet back when I heard a bullet slam against a rock in front of me and ricochet into the sky. I will never forget that noise. It was a high-pitched zinging noise and had a fade to the noise that seemed to go on forever until it finally dissipated and I could hear only the distant sound of machine-gun fire and the occasional twirling sound of air as the bullets flew overhead.

It must have given me a bit of a fright, because I put my head down to the ground and dragged my entire body against the earth, which slowed my crawl to twice as long to return to where my brothers and father were.

"Nida, you did so good," my father said as he wiped the dirt from my face and arms when I reached them.

I felt a sense of pride and could see how proud my big brothers were of me. My oldest brother carried the satchel of potatoes for me as we made our way through the brush and trees.

We left the tree line and headed back into the thick jungle toward where the Americans were hiding in the cave.

We did this for weeks. I would get the potatoes, and then we would give what we had scavenged to the Americans. This went on until one day while we had just left the cave, a patrol of Japanese soldiers stumbled across the cave and opened fire. The Americans fired back, and my father and brother both grabbed my hand and started running.

We had run through the jungle and reached the dirt path when I heard gunfire again and the Japanese yelling and the sound of running soldiers behind us. The air in my small lungs felt as if I was breathing fire with every step. My legs strained as I tried desperately to keep up. Machine-gun fire sounded even closer than it had only moments ago, and I could see the dirt fly up directly in front of me, along the path we were running on. My mind raced with fear and tried to run even faster. I forced my mind to tell my legs to move faster, but I couldn't go any faster. I could feel myself slowing down.

After only moments, the Japanese soldiers were right behind me. I ran off the path and into the dense, forested jungle and tripped over a vine, falling face-first to the ground. I could hear the footsteps of the running soldiers as they passed me and continued to follow my father and brothers. A single shot rang out, and I could hear the footsteps of the soldiers come to a halt. I heard a Japanese officer yell for my father to turn around.

I crawled out of the brush back onto the path and could see my father facing the soldiers with his arms raised high in the air. One soldier searched my father and struck him with the butt of his rifle in the back. He fell to his knees, and the soldier tied his hands behind his back.

On the path next to my father lay my oldest brother, Pedring. He had been shot in the back of the head. and a pool of blood surrounded him. My eyes started to tear, and I wiped them dry with my arm.

The soldiers stood my father and the other prisoners up and moved them along the side of the path to a clearing. I followed them and hid myself in the foliage from time to time to keep them from seeing me. Once they reached the clearing, the soldiers lined up the men and pointed their rifles at them. My father looked in my direction and gave me a smile and motioned with his head to leave. I was about to hide back in the brush when, without a word, the Japanese opened fire, killing all the men, including my father.

I saw my father get struck with a bullet in the chest and buckle over, falling to his death. I covered my mouth to keep from screaming and slowly backed my way deeper into the jungle.

Chapter 4

It was early, and my mother and I were the only ones awake. I remember that life at home was significantly different. My mother had just lost her two oldest sons and her husband, and was left with nothing. She had sold everything she could, and I, along with my brother, would be reduced to theft of merchants and begging the American GIs for some food or candy, which I would take and trade for food for the family.

But as the weeks turned into months, more of my siblings were killed off by the Japanese. On this one day, the Japanese barged into our hut and took my six brothers outside; David had left early that morning to try and get some rice. My mother and I ran outside and begged the Japanese not to take them, but a Japanese soldier backhanded my mother, knocking her to the ground.

They tied up my brothers, then lined them up, along with a few other military-aged boys, and started shooting them one by one. I watched in horror as five of my brothers were shot in the head. The soldier got to my last brother, and I jumped in front of him and started dancing. The soldier looked at me and started to laugh, along with a few of his buddies. He kicked my brother in the back, knocking him to the ground, and walked away. I had saved my brother. I ran up and hugged him as tight as I could.

After that day, life at home started getting even worse. My mother's venom grew in ferocity and would be directed solely at me.

"Leonida, why are you so ugly?" she would say.

I knew she was struggling to raise us, and I tried my best to be a good girl for her. But I would always seem to get into trouble with her for the smallest of things. When I was older, I realized that my father had showed me the most affection, and I was just a constant reminder that he was no longer with us. With my father gone and most of my family either killed by the Japanese or missing. we officially became the poorest family in our village. We became the brunt of others' ridicule and the butt of their jokes. There wasn't much that we could do about it. So, we let it be and suffered their ridicule and their wrath for the most part. My brother was the only one in our family who was respected and feared. No one would talk badly about us when he was around and for good reason.

After my brothers and father were shot some in the village had told us how the Japanese found us that day. Apparently the man Ontu, who my father went toe-to-toe with at my hut during the early part of the war, along with two others, one I didn't know and the other man who was always nice to me and my family, had been rounded up and had snitched on my father as being a soldier in the Filipino army.

When my brother heard this, he went mad with anger and went to the first guy's house and stabbed him repeatedly in the chest with a knife, killing him in broad daylight and threatening anyone who was there, telling them that if anyone said anything, they would be next. He then went to the other man's hut that night and did the same to him. But when he went to the last guy's hut I intervened and begged my brother not to kill him.

I arrived at this man's hut, and my brother had him on his knees with a knife to his throat.

"'No, David, please don't!" I velled.

My brother looked up at me as I approached and said, "He got Father killed."

I reached the two of them.

"He has always been good to us, and his family has always helped us when Father was away," I pleaded.

"But he turned our father over to the enemy," he said, turning his attention back to the man on his knees.

The man begged for his life and then he said something that I will never forget.

"The Japanese tortured us until we confirmed what Ontu had said about your father. I just couldn't take it anymore and said yes, he was in the army before the war."

"I don't see any marks of torture on you." my brother said as he once again put the blade to his throat.

"Check my back. They whipped me with bamboo until I wanted to die." he exclaimed.

My brother removed the knife from his throat and used it to cut his shirt off his back exposing the red and scabbed stripes along his back.

"You see, I didn't want to say anything. But Ontu went to the Japanese for favor- and the Japanese pressed us to confirm what Ontu had told them." he cried. –"I wish I could have withstood the pain, but it was just too much. I'm so sorry."

"Please. David. don't," I begged.

My brother walked around in front of him and leaned down, putting his face directly in front of his, and whispered something I couldn't hear and pointed at me.

The man looked at me and said, "Thank you. Leonida."

I just looked at the man as my brother stood up and came toward me. He grabbed my hand. and we returned home.

David became my protector and my father figure, watching out for me as the months of war surrounded and encompassed our village.

I suspected that he went after the Japanese who had shot Father, because on occasion, he would come back to our hut early in the morning covered in blood that was not his own. But I didn't say anything about it because part of me was proud of him for doing it to avenge our father and our fellow Filipinos. The atrocities that I witnessed at the hands and bayonets of the Japanese made me despise them. I witnessed them beheading prisoners, Americans, and Filipinos, and even witnessed the coldness of their hearts when they tossed infants into the air only to have them caught by a fellow soldier's bayonet.

No, no loss would I carry for these monsters, and if my brother could take one out here and there, I would support him.

Chapter 5

It was a hard time growing up during the war without a father there to protect us and provide for us, but when my mother got sick with malaria and tuberculosis, my life was about to get even more difficult.

The Americans had pushed back the Japanese past our village and had set up a few bases close by, which I would frequent as much as possible. I didn't speak much English back then and all I could come up with was to gesture with a salute or a thumbs-up and say, "GIs number one" and "Thank you, Joes." The Americans seemed to get a kick out of this little girl trying to communicate with them and would give me chocolate bars, after which I would run off and trade these for food for my family.

One day I came home from the American GI base and had a stick of Juicy Fruit chewing gum held tightly in my hand. One of the GIs gave it to me for a salute, and it smelled like nothing I had ever smelled before. As soon as the aroma hit my nostrils, I was tempted to open the tinfoil wrapping and eat it, but I figured I could probably make a better trade for it than I had for the chocolates I normally traded.

As I approached my village, I noticed a man leaving my hut as I was entering and he gave me a weird smile as he passed the open doorway and headed up the path through the village. I stopped and waited for him to leave before I went inside.

My mother was lying down in the front area of the hut, coughing and sweating. I asked where David was, and she told me she had sent him to the city of Porac for some medicine and that he wouldn't be back until the next day. I walked up to her and was about to offer her the chewing gum the American GIs gave me, when she pointed and told me to gather my bedroll and someone would be by to take me away.

I remember pleading with her not to get rid of me. but she swung the back of her hand at me. I dodged the strike and stood back out of

reach and cried for her not to get rid of me. "Please, Mama, I will be a good girl, I promise."

But my pleas landed on deaf ears, and she turned away from me and said, "Get your things together. They will be here soon to get you."

As I rolled up my bedroll and put on my burlap dress, the man who had smiled at me as I entered came in with a rather stern-looking woman. I stood in the doorway holding my bedroll and watched as the woman looked at me with disgust. I could feel her eyes penetrate me as she scanned me from head to foot. She let out a puff of air from her mouth when she met my eyes and nodded to the man. The man set a bag of rice down next to my mother and removed one hundred and twenty-five pesos and placed it in my mother's outstretched hand. My mother didn't look at me as the lady grabbed my hand and dragged me from the hut. I know because I watched her face until I couldn't see it anymore. She was focused on the coins in her hand the whole time I was being removed from my home.

I would soon realize that I had been sold into slavery just before my fourth birthday and for only a bag of rice and one hundred and twenty-five pesos, which was about seventy-five US cents, so my mother could pay for her medicine.

Even to this day I have never felt more betrayed, abandoned, and alone in my entire life.

Chapter 6

The war had been going on for over two years, and I had served one year with the Ventura-Fallow family as their slave and servant. I would work from sunup to past sundown both in their fields and at their home. I was mistreated by the lady of the house, Aggie, who usually beat me at least twice a week. I had grown accustomed to my new life, as much as any five-year-old could, and resigned to the fact that this was now my life. This was only after a few attempts to reunite with my family resulted in multiple lashes on my back and legs and removal of any food for days on end, with each attempt stretching out the length of withholding food.

I remember after four days without being fed, I would sneak off and scavenge a potato, just like my dad had taught me. I did what was demanded of me physically, but my mind was still my own.

As I stood in the cornfield picking the cobs, I watched the planes shoot at and circle one another in the air above me. I would often think of doing something with my life, and I knew that the only way that would happen was by going to America when they won this war.

I knew they would win the war because they were nice to me and they were the good guys. After all the atrocities I had witnessed of the Japanese soldiers treating my people worse than pigs in the slaughterhouse—tossing babies into the air and catching them with the ends of their bayonets; the beheadings, so many beheadings; and the senseless killings—no, the Americans would have to win this war because I didn't want to be in a world where people treated us like the Japanese did.

The night at my new residence was especially terrifying for me, and I shiver to talk about it now. I was set at the end of a small room that had only one wall that was connected to the house and faced the courtyard, which was in the middle of the house. It had a roof that sloped toward the courtyard. But it often leaked in the rain, and I would have to push myself up against the wall of the house to keep from sleeping in a puddle.

Since my bed was no more than some thick cardboard-like material. I would usually wake up wet from the bed absorbing the moisture.

The spring and summer months were especially bad because the mosquitoes would always attack me in my sleep, causing me to wake up and shake them off me. Luckily. the man of the house, who I called the Mister. saw that my hands had swollen to almost twice their size from being bitten when I brought him his morning coffee; he came back that evening with mosquito netting to place around my bed. I was very thankful for that and made sure the Mister got his coffee first every mornino.

I wasn't the only servant the Ventura-Fallow family had at the house, although I was definitely the youngest and the only female servant they had, which meant that at night I would wake up to men touching me and wanting to kiss me. I stabbed one of the older farmhands in the shoulder with a sharpened stick one night. and he left me alone for a while anyway.

But as soon as I had a mosquito net around my bed, I tied cans and metal to the bottom of it, and it would clang and clatter if someone tried to get to me. It went off for a few nights and woke everyone up. and I could hear the farm supervisor yell to leave me alone. Unfortunately, the threat of a supervisor wasn't much of a deterrent and a few nights later the loud clank of the metal and cans woke me but this time the Mister came out to investigate the noise and caught the guy walking back to his bedroll. He was told to leave right then and Mister yelled at the supervisor. I had never seen the supervisor look so scared. He looked just like the other field hands and that's when I think I realized that he was afraid I would say something about what he tried to do to me. I never did say anything because after that night the supervisor made sure the clatter from my netting never rang again while I slept.

I can remember that I had the stick of Juicy Fruit gum under my pillow and even though the strong smell that it once held was gone, a faint smell of it still lingered. When things would get bad for me at the Ventura-Fallow house. I would hold it to my nose at night and it would calm me creating a soothing feeling as I thought of times before I was here with this family.

I held on to the stick of gum for another year or so until the Missus found it and took it away. I told myself that it didn't matter, but looking back, I realize that by taking it away, she had removed the last bit of who I used to be.

Chapter 7

I acclimated to my new life as the years passed. I would shuck corn until my fingers bled, tend to the pigs and chickens. and clean and serve the Mister; his wife, Aggie the Missus; and their daughter, Consita Fallow.

Consita was about four years older than I was, and she was nice to me but wouldn't stay around me too long because her mother would reprimand her and punish me for socializing.

My life had turned hard and painful. Even with the added years to my age, I would still get beaten by the Missus at least once a month for minor offenses, sometimes even without provocation.

I would work the fields by day and be a house servant by night. I knew my role and worked diligently at every task for fear of a lashing from the Missus. I was even trusted with going to the market for the family—supervised, of course, by the Missus, but it was a nice break from the hard labor of the fields.

Occasionally, I would run into my brother David, who would try and sneak a conversation in when the Missus was busy bartering with a merchant. I don't know how he always managed to be there on the day we went to the market, but there he was, every time.

He would always ask, "How are you, Nida?" And I would always reply with the same answer: "I'm good. They are good to me." I knew what my brother was capable of doing, and I liked the Mister too much for him to be dead.

We would only have a little time, but that's all that was needed for me to feel better. He would always say, "You hang tough, Nida. When I'm older, I will come and get you." I simply nodded and caught up with the Missus.

We never talked about our mother. I never asked, and he never offered any information about her. It was a silent question that neither of us wanted to address.

While working in the fields I would often think of my father and would imagine us walking down to the market. It was starting to get difficult to remember his face, and I felt bad about not being able to see his face in my mind anymore. I could remember it when I remembered going to the market with him which is why I tried to imagine us at the market. But as the years progressed, it became more difficult to remember his face. There was another instance where I could remember my father's face vividly, but I didn't like to think about that. I'm referring to the day he was killed by the Japanese. I will never forget that for as long as I live. And I would only think of that day when I couldn't remember my father's face at all.

I saw very little progress with my life as the years passed. The Missus saw to that. With her venomous words, she could strike at my core, adding physiological and physical pain. But I wouldn't let her win. I was a Clarete, and I wanted nothing more than to show her I was stronger than her, even at the young age of seven years old.

I guess I was about thirteen years old when I was finally allowed to attend school. I struggled with learning and didn't like it very much. The other kids far surpassed me, and I would be made fun of by other students for being dumb. The teachers weren't much better. They would say, "Why are you even here?" and "Why are you trying to learn? You're a servant girl."

It was a humiliating time, and I dreaded the walk home. The other kids were in better shape than I was and would often tease me on the way home and even push me down or gang up on me and beat me.

I remember this one girl who kept shoving my back all the way to the entrance of the Fallow home, only to slice me with a sharp stick and beat me in front of my home.

The Mister saw this and chased the girl away as I lay bleeding in the mud. The Mister picked me up and carried me inside.

"You'll be okay, little one," he said as he laid me down on a real bed inside a small room in the house. He had one of the older servants tend to my wounds and feed me meat with my rice. He brought in my two dresses from my space in the courtyard and said, "This is your room now," and set them down on a dresser.

The next morning, I could hear an argument between the Mister and Missus. It didn't last long though. The Mister raised his voice, and the argument seemed to stop at that point. Shortly after, the Missus opened the door to the room and poked her head inside and said, "You will no longer work in the field. You are to come with us to the restaurant today, so get dressed." She closed the door, and I could hear her walk away.

Chapter 8

I worked in the restaurant for three more years. I started out doing dishes. emptying garbage. and clearing tables. I didn't make any money for the work, but I did start to eat a lot better, having meat with almost every meal.

I never returned to school, which I was grateful for. I worked from sunup to well past sundown every day. I would get a half day off on Sunday but only because the restaurant wasn't open for breakfast on Sundays.

After about two years of dishes and garbage, I was allowed to help prepare the food. The main chef liked me and called me beautiful. I had never been called that before, and I liked it. He was kind to me, and he would sneak me special food from time to time when I was washing dishes.

I remember this one day when the restaurant was packed with visitors, primarily from the navy base, and it was mostly because it was raining outside. The Missus told me to run to the market and get some supplies. On my way back from the market, I ran into the girl who pushed me all the way home when I was in school. I stopped dead in my tracks as she rode up the street on her bike toward me.

She was a little taller now, but so was I. As she got closer. I could tell that I had a little more weight on me than I had three years ago, and I set the supplies down on the ground by my feet.

The girl stopped her bike, and the two girls who were with her stopped as well. She started saying mean things to me and tried to bully me, but I stood my ground and just stared at her.

"What? Are you so stupid and ugly that you forgot how to speak?" she said as she got off her bike and took a couple of steps toward me.

A rage built up in me, and I didn't wait for her to get all the way to me before I ran at her and started hitting her in the face.

She fell to the ground crying, and I turned my attention toward her friends and walked toward them. They quickly turned their bikes around and pedaled away, leaving their friend to fend for herself.

I saw her try to get up from the ground, and I said, "If you get up, it will be the last time you ever get up again."

Our eyes met, and she sat back on the ground, sobbing. "I'm sorry, Nida- I'm sorry.'

I slowly walked up to her and then walked right past her. I grabbed my supplies and looked down at her, and without saying a word, I walked away and headed back to the restaurant.

I felt like a champion. I felt vindicated. Then, as I almost reached the restaurant, the emotions started to build, and I started to feel a little bad. I stood outside the restaurant and composed myself.

I had stood up for myself and was proud of it, but while I was standing in front of the restaurant, I realized that that wasn't who I was.

I don't start fights, I thought to myself. I'm not the bad people. I'm not like the Japanese.

I looked through the window of the restaurant and watched as all the American service men ate their food, and I thought, I'm like the Americans. I'm the good guy.

I took a vow to never start a fight again, and to this day, I never have. I walked into the restaurant and went back to helping the chef in the kitchen.

I started to enjoy my job at the restaurant and even started making a little bit of money. Yes, I was actually getting paid by the people who had purchased me for PI 25. The Missus was still mean to me, but

she was so busy at the restaurant, and now that I was in the kitchen, where the chef wouldn't allow anyone who wasn't supposed to be in there, we rarely saw each other during the day.

It was during this time that I started to notice men as more than father figures. I started to enjoy their advances and the kind words they would say to me. I was turning seventeen at the end of the next month and my hormones were a little erratic.

I would flirt with the American sailors and marines when they would come in for their meals if time permitted, and only if I knew that the Missus wasn't anywhere within sight or earshot. Some Filipino men would try to talk with me, but I wasn't interested in them. I was drawn to and attracted to the white American men. Maybe it was because the Americans were always so nice to me on the base when I was a child and here in the restaurant, or maybe it was because I was treated so poorly by my own Filipino people.

There was one man that struck me right away. He had a great smile and was in really good shape. He would come in about once a week with some friends and order the same thing every time, rice and lumpia with a Coke. Charles was in the marine corps, and I was captivated with him immediately.

Chapter 9

After the days turned to weeks and weeks turned into a month, my door opened, and the Mister stood in the doorway to my small room.

"Nida, I need to see you in the front room. Get dressed quickly, and meet me there," he said as he closed the door behind him as he left.

It was late. The sun had been up for at least an hour or so, and I was still asleep. I'm in trouble, I thought as I quickly dressed and headed out of my room to receive my punishment.

I turned the corner from the hallway and entered the front living room. My brother David was standing by the Mister. I wanted to run to him and give him a hug, but I stood at the entrance of the living room with my hands folded in front of the other and looked down at the ground as I had been instructed to do when summoned for my entire life with them.

Water filled my eyes, and the ground got blurry. No one spoke for a few seconds, and then the Mister said, "Nida, come here.'

I walked over to him and looked up at him and saw my brother walk up to me.

"You are free to go," the Mister said.

His words echoed in my mind, and I didn't understand until my brother walked up to me and grabbed me by the shoulders, looking me directly in my tear-filled eyes, and said, "Nida, you are free, and you're coming home with me."

I stood there for a moment, and the tears ran down my face.

"1 can leave?" I asked the Mister, and he nodded his agreement.

I looked around the room and didn't see the Missus or their daughter anywhere.

"1 can leave?" I asked again.

My brother stepped aside and motioned toward the door. "Go get your things. and you can come live with me."

I looked up at the Mister. and he had a half smile across his face and kept nodding his head in agreement.

It hit me like a bolt of lightning. I was free to go. I was a free woman. I grabbed my brother and sobbed on his shoulder. I hugged him so tight, and he returned the embrace in kind. We held each other for a minute or so before I broke the embrace and said, "I will go and get my things."

I ran to my room and opened the door. I looked around the room and went under the mattress that was on the floor. I pulled out and quickly counted my seventy-five pesos and put them in my pocket. I started grabbing my clothes. I had two shirts a worn flower dress that didn't quite fit, and two pairs of slacks. I quickly gathered them up and looked around the room. I had nothing else.

This was the moment that would haunt me for the rest of my life. I had nothing, literally. The clothes I was holding in my hand were hand-me-downs from the daughter. I owned nothing. I put the clothes on the mattress and walked out of the room.

My brother noticed me standing in the hallway and asked, -'Where are your things?"

I looked up at him and said, •'1 don't have anything that is mine.

My brother looked at me with a half-turned head and then looked at the Mister. The Mister's half smile waned from his face as my brother stared at him. I could see my brother turn toward the Mister and I

said. "I have some money I earned in my pocket. and that's all I want to bring with me.

This stopped my brother from walking toward the Mister and he turned to me and said- "Then let's go home."

The Mister just stood there—no goodbye, no nothing. I had served him for over thirteen years, and he could say nothing to me as I walked out their door and out of their lives forever. My brother reached for my hand, and we left the Ventura-Fallow home.

Chapter 10

My brother had a small place near the navy base in Subic Bay, and I lived there with him for close to a year. I took a job working as a waitress in one of the clubs and started making some good money with the tips from the American sailors and marines.

It did take me some time to adjust to my newfound freedom. and my brother was very patient with me. It is difficult to explain how much being a servant can mess with your mind. You feel less than human at times. And when something like freedom is presented, you don't feel as if you are deserving of it. It is uncomfortable and very much the scariest feeling one could feel.

As the months slowly progressed, I found myself again and thrived on making the most of my freedom. I worked hard every day and even worked double shifts to make some extra money. But when I wasn't working or there weren't any extra hours to pick up, I would get lonely. And as I sat alone in my brother's house, I would often wonder if this was all still a dream.

I would wonder what my Mister and Missus were doing and how they were getting their daily needs met. I couldn't help it—they were the only life I had known for the past thirteen years. But I also couldn't shake the feeling that the Mister was not doing well without me and that I should go by his restaurant and check on him. But my brother warned me about going back until I was truly ready to face them as my own free woman. He was right, of course. Even though I would think about them often, I wouldn't be able to truly face them, especially the Missus, until I was able to forgive her for all she had put me through.

After nearly a year, I was working at the club as usual when someone very familiar walked in and sat down at my table. His blue eyes stared at mine smiling at me without a smile across his lips. As I approached him his lips parted, showing a white smile as his eyes slowly squinted. His gaze melted my heart and it felt familiar and it felt right.

It was Charles, and he was all alone, sitting at my table. And the best part was that he hadn't come here to eat. He came to see me. He just came back from America, and he stopped by the Ventura-Fallow restaurant to see me.

"When you weren't there, I asked Ben where you went, and he told me that you were here," Charles said.

The club was pretty busy, but I made as many trips by Charles as I could to talk with him. Right before my shift ended, he asked to see me after work. I said yes, of course, and we met out in front of the club and just walked and talked for hours.

I didn't want the night to ever end. But he had to get back to the base, and I needed to get some sleep before my morning shift. However, as he walked me to my brother's house, he asked me to dinner the next night. I said yes immediately, and he leaned in and gave me my very first kiss.

It was amazing. His lips were soft, and he was so gentle. It wasn't a long kiss. I would have liked to kiss him again, but he said, "Good night, my Nida," and turned and walked away.

I thought of him all night. I was infatuated with him. He was in the marine corps and he was tall and he looked really strong. And while I was in bed, deep in sleep, I dreamed of his kiss.

The next day, he took me onto the base, and he took me to an American restaurant they had there. It was really good food, a little greasy but the flavors were great, and they put so much on the plate that I could only eat half of it.

After dinner, we walked around the base, and I met his commanding officer and platoon lieutenant. They were very nice to me, calling me ma'am and just saying really nice things to me.

We dated for a few weeks, and I fell in love with him. He was charming, polite, and caring, and he would come over every chance

he could. My brother really liked him, which helped me trust him even more. But after a month of dating, he told me that he was going to be returning to the United States in a couple of weeks. I was crushed. I had found a man that could take care of me—and he really loved me and I him—yet I was about to lose the only love that I had ever known. We were at the base when he told me the news and I can remember crying softly and him gently wiping the tears from my face.

"I don't want to lose you, Nida," he said. "You're my Nida, and I want you to marry me and take you back to the States with me."

But the rules for military men were very clear about marriage, and we both knew it. American service men were not allowed to marry Filipino women, although a few navy sailors did marry, the marine corps was very strict about this policy. No marine had married a Filipino woman, ever.

Just then Charles's commanding officer came by and noticed I was crying and approached us. When he inquired about my tears, Charles explained to him that he had proposed to me. The commanding officer excused himself, along with Charles, and they walked off to talk.

They were talking softly and talked for about ten minutes. I could see Charles gesturing with his hands, and then he put his hands by his side as the commanding officer spoke. It got really quiet for a few minutes before I heard a very loud "Yes, sir!" This grabbed my attention, and I saw his commanding officer walk away and saw Charles turn and run toward me.

"Nida, Nida!" he yelled as he ran to me. "He said yes. He said we could get married."

I was overjoyed with happiness—more than I had ever been in my entire life. He got down on one knee and took my hand and proposed properly right there. I naturally said yes, and we kissed and held each other for a long while.

Chapter 11

We got married on the base by the navy chaplain. My husband wore his dress blues and I had on a white flowing dress that he had bought for me. It was the happiest day of my life to that point, and as we walked away from the altar as husband and wife, we were walking under crossed swords held by his marine friends. Just before we got to the last pair of marines with the swords crossed overhead, they dropped them blocking us from passing, and I felt a swat on my butt from the sword behind me.

The last marines once again raised their swords and I heard one of them say "Welcome to the marine corps." And then my new husband led me out of the church and we left for our honeymoon.

A week later my husband kissed me goodbye, and he boarded the ship. He promised to send for me as soon as he could arrange it. I waved goodbye as the ship left the dock and I stayed until I couldn't see the ship any longer.

I went back to my brother's house and went back to work at the club. Days passed and no word from him. Then days turned into weeks without a word and then weeks turned to months. I had tried to go to the base and contact him but no one there could help me track him down back in the States.

My coworkers began to mock me and started to put doubt in my mind as to whether he would be sending for me. At first it was just a little doubt but after a few more weeks of them saying these things. I truly started to feel that he had forgotten about me.

One day my coworker just walked up to me and gave me a hug. She said, "I'm so sorry he did this to you. Nida." I cried on her shoulder, and we hugged for a few minutes. After my shift I walked home thinking that I had been abandoned once again, and I started to cry. I remember talking to myself and saying out loud, "Why do people treat me this way?"

I cried all the way home, but when I turned the corner to go to my house, I saw a military jeep parked out in front. As I approached, I saw two marines sitting inside. They got out of the jeep when I got to my door and they asked if I was Leonida Clarete.

When I said yes, one of the marines removed an envelope from his coat pocket and handed it to me. I looked at it and then looked up at the two marines and said. "I'm sorry, but I don't know how to read."

One of the marines smiled at me and said, "Ma'am, this is a plane ticket to the United States and a note from your husband Charles. Would you like me to read it to you?"

I said yes, and he read the note. "My dearest Nida, I'm sorry it has taken so long to get you to my side. I can't wait to hold you in my arms once again. Love, Charles."

Tears ran down my face, and I hugged the marine that read the letter to me. Then I hugged the other one and said, "Thank you, thank you!"

Then the other marine said something I found hilarious: "Wow, thanks. ma'am. Would you like me to read it again?" The marine that read me the note smacked the other on the arm and we all laughed.

I asked. "When do I leave?" And he said, "Tomorrow morning, ma'am, we will be here at zero eight hundred to collect you and bring you on the base for your flight."

I packed up that night and shared my good news with my brother David. He was so happy for me and I was really going to miss him. After I packed up my suitcases, I grabbed my ticket and headed back to my work. I showed my friends the ticket. Some seemed envious, the same ones that told me "he isn't coming for you," but a couple seemed to be genuinely happy for me.

My boss said that he would really miss me and went to the cash register and paid me twice what my normal pay was. "America is expensive, Nida." he said with a smile and gave me a hug. I said my goodbyes, and I left for home.

I couldn't sleep at all that night. I was too excited to sleep. I tried to fall asleep again and again, but I just couldn't, so I got up and cleaned my brother's house.

My brother came home around six in the morning and we ate breakfast and talked until the knock on the door came. I gave him a hug and he handed me some money. I tried to refuse it, but he insisted. He picked up my suitcases and we headed outside.

The two marines quickly took the suitcases from my brother and loaded them into the jeep. I hugged my brother again and the marines helped me into the jeep. As we drove away, I could see my brother wave with the biggest smile I had ever seen across his face.

It didn't take long for us to get to the base and before I knew it, I was loaded onto a big ship and was headed to San Francisco. The trip took almost three days. But once I arrived in San Francisco, I was put aboard an airplane, and before I knew it, we were airborne and on our way to Kansas City, Missouri. I had never flown and it was an exhilarating feeling. But it quickly went away once we reached a level altitude. The stewardesses were very nice and brought me a meal and a soda.

After I ate the meal. I grew really tired and closed my eyes. One of the stewardesses gave me a pillow and a blanket and I fell fast asleep.

I awoke to the captain speaking over the intercom. "We will be arriving in ten minutes."

I looked around and other people were just waking up as well. The stewardess took my pillow and blanket and asked me to put my seat upright and to make sure my seat belt was fastened. I did as I was instructed and waited as the exhilarating feeling came back upon our descent. The tires hit the tarmac, and we slowed to a stop. The door was opened and a ladder was pushed up to the opening. When I got off the plane, it was bright out, and I couldn't see well. So, I closely followed the people in front of me until my eyes adjusted to the light. I walked to where people were directing me to go for my suitcases and as I approached the area, I saw Charles and an older man and a lady with him.

I ran full speed and jumped into his arms, wrapping my legs around him and giving him a strong kiss. I was so happy to see him. As he lowered me back to the ground, he kissed me one more time and said, "Welcome to America." He introduced me to his parents who were really nice to me, and both of them gave me a hug.

I had made it. I had come from a land of servitude to the land of the free. What would happen from here was up to me, and I planned to make the most of it, which I did.

Volume II

Chapter 1

Survive

I had been a little nervous to meet Charlie's parents, but they were wonderful people. They loved me and I loved them. I even called them Mom and Dad. I married Charlie for love not for money, so I was surprised when I arrived and discovered that his parents were rich. They gave me everything. I liked being married to Charlie very much. He obviously loved me. The military took his stripes when we got married and he sent for me as soon as he could, so that proves it. When I arrived with baby Janet, we all lived at his parent's house, but they soon bought us a nice little two- bedroom house.

When I came to the US, I didn't know how to dress or have proper manners. America was very different from the Philippines in so many ways. I didn't even know how to sleep on a bed because I'd never had one before. Every night, I'd lay down to sleep on the floor and then Charlie would pick me up and put me on the bed until I learned how to fall asleep in one. I also worked hard to learn English, but people kept teaching me swear words because they thought it was funny. One day Charlie's father gave me a spanking because I said some bad words, but it was innocent. I didn't know what they meant. In the end, Charlie's parents sent me to a school where they taught me how to dress and all those things you need to know. I enjoyed learning all those things. They even paid for a mole to be removed from my face. The doctor did a great job and I didn't get a scar.

Charlie was handsome and rich, so there were always girls who liked him. I didn't understand why he would like me enough to marry me when there are so many pretty girls around. So, one day I asked him.

"Charlie, why do you like me?"

"Because you're funny and you're nice. And you always tell the truth,"

We had children together — Janet and Charles, who we called Chuck. They were so cute and adorable, but sometimes they were mischievous. There was one time when they were really little that they decided to go visit their grandparents. I think Janet was around five years old and Chuck was about two years old. While I was talking with someone on the phone, they decided to walk to their grandma's house. So they just walked out the door and down the street! Chuck didn't even have a diaper on, so his ding-dong was hanging out and everything! If I hadn't been so scared when I realized they were gone, I would have thought it was very cute. They were holding hands and happily walking down the road and they didn't even know which way to go. Luckily, their great-grandma saw them and brought them home. We asked them what they were doing and Janet said they were going to visit grandma. I spanked them good for that one!

When John Kennedy was president, I met his brother, Robert. He came to give a speech at the Kansas City Courthouse, so I went there with my kids. I even got to talk with him. I'm not scared of anybody and I'm a friendly person, so I just walked right up to him and started talking to him. He was very handsome and charming. He was so nice and listened very patiently to me while I chattered, although I don't think he really understood most of what I said. He even gave me a rose. I was so happy and wanted to talk with him some more, but he couldn't stay long. In June of 1968, when I heard he was killed, I was so sad. I wanted to go to New York for his funeral, but I couldn't. I couldn't afford the trip and on top of that I had two kids to take care of. I couldn't drag them that far and I definitely couldn't just leave them at home. I'm their mom, so it's my job to take care of them, not someone else's. Even today, I remember meeting him and how nice he was. I can't forget that. When people are nice to me, I can't forget them. I don't know why, I just can't.

My mother-in-law, Viola, asked me to perm her hair one day and I was happy to do it. It turned out great, so she bragged to all her friends about what a wonderful job I did perming her hair and they wanted me to do theirs, too. I really liked doing that and decided I wanted to learn how to be a real beauty technician.

I went to Viola and said, "l want to go to beauty school so I can be a real beauty technician."

"l don't know," she said. "That might be hard to do."

"l really want to try, though."

"Well, if you can find a school to take you, I'll pay for you to do it."

I got my friend, Ann, to take me around to all the beauty schools in the area. She had blonde hair and blue eyes and was very sweet and pretty.

I'd go in and say, "l want to take classes."

"Ok, no problem. Fill out this form."

I would sit down with Ann, who would fill out the form for me since I wasn't good at writing yet. Everything would be fine except for the question about where I went to school because, of course, I couldn't go to school when I was growing up. We'd fill out the rest of the form, though, and give it to the receptionist, who would look it over.

"You didn't fill out where you went to school," she'd say.

"I grew up in the Philippines and couldn't go to school," I'd reply.

"What kind of school do you think we are? We only take educated people here.

We don't let just anybody in here! We won't accept you."

Every school I'd go to, they'd say the same thing. They wouldn't take me because I didn't graduate from a school. Eventually, we got to the last one. This time, though, I was smart.

"I want to take classes," I said to the receptionist.

"Ok, no problem. Fill out this form."

Ann sat down with me and we started filling out the form. This time, when we got to the education question, I told her to write down that I went to the Republic Center in the Philippines. This time, when I handed it to the receptionist, she glanced over the paper, saw that it was all filled in, and told me I was accepted. I got so excited that I was accepted that I jumped around in happiness, like a little kid.

"Don't jump, Nida!" Ann exclaimed. "Act like you know what you're doing!

Just like that, I was admitted to a beauty school! The whole time I was studying there, I was scared that they'd find out I made up attending college in the Philippines and I'd get kicked out, but they never found out and in the end I graduated!

One of the first things I did when I got accepted was find a really good teacher. Her name was Ruby. Normally, all the students would take classes together and read a lot of books and things, but I knew that I would have trouble doing that. I saw Ruby working there and liked how she did things, so I approached her.

"Hi," I said. "My name is Nida. I'm a student here now, but I want a private teacher."

"Not me," she said. "l have to work another job to have enough money to pay my bills and take care of my kids. I can't afford to teach anyone."

"I'll pay you three times the normal teacher's pay, so then you can quit your other job and just teach me."

"Three times the rate? Really?"

"Yes."

Ok, then. Let's do it."

I went home after that and told Viola that I had a private teacher and told her how much I was paying Ruby per hour. She said ok. She never even questioned the amount. I worked so hard for the next several months and graduated early. It was so hard because I couldn't read well and had to learn everything by just doing it. The first shop I worked for was in a Macy's store. Our school had us go to a training shop when we first graduated and this is the one they set me up with. I was having too much trouble at first, so they had me go back to the school for some more training in hair design. I even came up with my own hair design. I called it Piccadelio.

I was mostly happy being married to Charlie, except that I love to travel and he didn't like to take me anywhere. He was very nice to me. The big problem was that women loved him because he was charismatic. One day, Ann called to tell me she saw Charlie's car in Lover's Lane. Charlie was very proud of his car and it was easy to recognize. I was angry when I heard that, but wanted to see for myself, so she offered to drive me out to Lover's Lane. I took a hammer with me, just in case. It wasn't hard for us to find his car there, so we parked nearby. I grabbed the hammer I had brought with me and stalked over to peer in the windows. There he was, making out with a young woman like he wasn't a married man with two kids at home! I started pounding his car with the hammer, swinging it with all my might while the woman screamed and Charlie yelled at me to stop.

"Charlie! How dare you kiss another woman like that, when you are married and have two children!"

"I didn't know he was married," the woman cried.

"Charlie," I said, "let me see your hand."

He showed me his hand and I could see that he had taken off his ring so the woman wouldn't know he was married.

"Since you didn't know," I told her, "We'll take you home. I don't have an issue with you since he lied about being married."

As she shakily got out of the car, I told her to be careful of the broken glass on the ground and pointed her to Ann's car. I continued to beat up his beloved car and then I told Charlie not to bother coming home. I was kicking him out. Once is enough. I'm not stupid and I know that if you cheat once, you're going to cheat again. So when he begged me to take him back, I said no. I even called the police on him when he didn't want to leave.

We ended up getting divorced. He wanted to take our children away from me, but I wouldn't allow that. He even got a lawyer. They came to my house and threatened to take away the children, but I told them that I would never allow my children to be parted from me. I was sold into slavery and there was no way I would ever allow my children to be taken away. I'm not someone who will give away their children and forget about them. They're my children. I told them to leave before I called the police and that if he kept trying to take the kids away, either he'd have to kill me or I'd kill him. So they left in a hurry and I got to keep them.

We had to talk to each other sometimes because of the kids. He asked if he could see them regularly and naturally, I knew he loved them.

"Of course you can see them," I told him. "They're your kids, too. But you can't see them here, at my house. I'll have someone drive them to your mom's and you can see them there."

I said that because I still loved his mom and knew that she loved me, too. She had wanted me to stay married to Charlie, but she understood me.

Isn't that something? Lots of couples fight a lot when they get divorced, but we didn't. I didn't bother him and he didn't bother me, even about the kids. Most people cry when they get divorced, but not me. I didn't even cry once. I think God was protecting my heart. The marriage was done, so why cry? I've got kids to support so I don't have time for that. We both eventually got married again. I don't have to hate him because of what he did to me. It's in the past. God will take care of that.

The last time I took the kids to see him and his parents was when my second husband, Sherman, was re-stationed and we were moving to Oregon. Charlie didn't really fight hard for the kids after that, and when he sent money for child support, it was only a little bit and not regularly. I got to keep the house when we divorced, but when I remarried I signed it over to him.

Charlie's parents worked hard to stay in their grandchildren's lives. One year Sherman and I took all our kids to see them at Christmas. They had presents for their own grandchildren but not the others. So little Jason said, "Where is my present?" They were very little kids, so they couldn't understand. So, they went and bought presents for the rest of the kids as well. They were always good to all the kids. They were good people, very good people. They hadn't wanted to see us divorce and they said I would always be their daughter-in-law.

"Take care of them, Sherman," Viola said. "Because I love them."

Chapter 2

New Love

I met my second husband, Sherman, at a party in Kansas City, Missouri. He was in the Air Force and stationed nearby. This was in 1966. My friend invited me to a party at her house, but I told her I couldn't go because of the kids. So, she told me to bring them with me and they could play in the other room, so I did. It was a fun evening and Sherman was staring at me the whole night. My friend teased me that he liked me, but I didn't believe her at first. What handsome, single man would like a divorced woman with little kids? It turned out Sherman did!

One time, we were on a date to the river. It was nice being together, just the two of us. We couldn't get away together very often because I worked and had two kids.

While we were at the river, I waded into the water and over to a rock.

"Watch this," I told Sherman. "I'll catch a fish for you."

I saw a fish near the rock and I caught it with my hands and tossed it onto the ground. He was so surprised!

"How did you do that?" he asked.

"That's how we did it in the Philippines when I was a kid. If you couldn't do that, you couldn't eat."

Sherman started coming over all the time to see me and play with my kids. I could see that he was a good man who cared a lot about my children. One day, I decided to take the kids to the beach. I got a hotel room there so we could have lots of fun playing in the water. Sherman was working swing shift at the time, so he got off at around 2 o'clock a.m. He didn't know I had decided to take the kids to the beach, so I called to let him know that I wasn't at home. He drove the two hours to come be with us. I found out later that he'd bet the other GIs in his Air Force unit that he'd get me to sleep with him while we were there. He must have thought I had called him to invite him to sleep with me! Those guys made money off of Sherman for that one! My father had told me to not sleep with men unless we are married, so I always followed that rule. I wasn't going to shack up with anyone and in the end Sherman gave up and went back to work at the base. He was so mad that he didn't call me again for two weeks. He was hoping I would call him, but I wasn't going to give in on this. One day, I happened to look down and see a big, fat, four-leaf clover. I picked it to admire it, and just then the phone rang. It was Sherman, calling to say that he would marry me after all. I said, Ok, let's do it.

We got married two months after we met. I could tell Sherman was a good man, especially because my kids liked him. One day, I left Janet and Chuck with a neighbor while Sherman and I went on a date in Oberlin Park. We had already gotten our marriage license and, while we were at the park, Sherman said "let's go get married right now!" I just laughed because it was obviously a joke. I had already been married once, so I know that weddings are big and exciting and the bride wears a white dress. I didn't know anything about this thing called "eloping."

We found a preacher outside a church working in the yard and asked him ho much it would be to marry us. He said it would be $10, but Sherman only had $8 with him.

"Can I pay you $5 today and the rest on Friday when I get paid?" he asked. "That will be fine," the preacher replied.

So, the minister invited MIO people as witnesses and married us right then and there; but all the time I still think it's just a big joke because it's nothing like my first wedding. I didn't find out the truth until we were leaving and Sherman opened the car door for me.

"Get in, Mrs. Watson," he said.

I stared at him. "Why are you calling me Mrs. Watson? Wasn't this just a joke?"

"No."

I ran back inside and found the preacher.

"Are we married for real? It's not just a joke?" I asked.

He got mad. "No it's not a joke! Why would you think I would marry people as a joke? Did you not really want to get married? Did he trick you?"

I told him it was ok and went back to the car. But I still couldn't believe I was really married! We went to White Castle for our wedding dinner and had fifteen cent hamburgers.

Janet and Chuck were at a neighbor's house while we were eloping. When we got home that night, I brought them back home with me like usual because I wouldn't let them be apart from me even for one night. They were still very young, about six and three. They liked Sherman a lot and I liked him because he is a good man who takes good care of his friends. He even worked three jobs to help take care of the kids and I. That's why I was happy to marry him.

Our first child was born while we were still in Missouri. We had talked about names and Sherman liked Lydia for a girl. I liked the name too, but I could only pronounce it "Leja," so that's what we named her.

There was one time when the lady next door asked me to do her hair. She said that if I did her hair, she would drive me when I needed a ride somewhere. I agreed with her suggestion, so we set a date for the haircut. Our kids were playing together for a while, but then Janet started arguing with the neighbor's son. I could hear them from the other room, but I didn't get involved.

"Well, my mom is not gonna take your mom anywhere!" the boy yelled at Janet.

"Well then my mom is not gonna do your mom's hair!" she shouted back.

So he got even more upset and ran to his mother and said "Mom, her mom said she's not gonna do your hair no more!"

Instead of doing the right thing and coming to ask me what was going on, she went straight to Sherman and told him some story about Janet that wasn't entirely true. Sherman got upset and starts to blame Janet. I'm in the other room just listening to what they're saying, but I don't say anything, even though Janet has already told me what had really happened. I didn't say anything, but I think to myself just wait…I'm gonna get you when you leave here. I know my daughter and I know that she's telling the truth, but Sherman believed the neighbor because she's an adult, so he spanks Janet with a belt. The woman is happy and goes to leave. As soon as she leaves the house, I pounce on her and we started arguing. We're screaming at each other. Her husband hears the noise and comes running. He doesn't try to stop us, though. A crowd gathered and two men started grabbing baseball bats and swinging at each other. It was crazy! We all ended up talking things out once we calmed down, and everything was fine after she apologized for lying to Sherman and blaming Janet for everything. I forgave her, but told her that next time she should talk to me - mother to mother.

"You know I will protect my kids like you do," I told her, "but we need to talk these things out as mothers and leave the men out of it. We shouldn't be fighting like this. Even though things were fine after that, I was still mad that my daughter had gotten a spanking for nothing.

I asked Sherman to teach me how to drive. One of the men on base saw me and yelled: "You've got no business driving!" Sherman was upset for me, but he decided maybe the guy was right when I drove into another car!

Sherman took the blame, claiming he was driving when the base police approached us. His Commanding Officer believed him about who was driving and told him he could not drive on the base for three weeks. Three days later in a military court, the judge, who didn't like the CO, changed it to one week. So he only had to get a ride to work for that week.

In early 1968, Sherman was stationed at KC Fields in Klamath Falls, Oregon. It wasn't too long before our son, Jason, joined our family. I was pregnant twice while we were living in Klamath Falls, but I kept working right up until the babies were born. My boss and co-workers kept teasing me all the time for working so long. They said if I went into labor, they would roll me down the road to the hospital! One time, my shirt got too tight because the baby was so big, so I cut slits in the shirt so it would fit better.

My boss saw me and asked what I was doing, so I told him. He laughed and told me the baby would grow through the slits. They were so funny! I had a good time working with them.

At one point, I worked in the mess hall at the base. One day my boss told me to wipe down a light hanging over the tables.

"I'm not gonna do that," I said. "I have a dress on and you want me to climb up so the GIs can look up my skirt!"

"Don't argue and just do it!" she commanded.

"No! They're eating and they can all just go over and look up and see my panties!"

"If you don't go up there, you're going to be fired. Do you understand that?"

"Why don't you go up there yourself? You've got a big butt for them to look at!"

All the GIs laughed when I said that, but I was still angry. Then I remembered I'm a beauty operator. I still have all my supplies since I always brought them along when we moved.

"You said I'm fired, so I'm out of here!" I yelled. "I'll find a better job somewhere else where they treat me right!" So I left just like that and let her deal with the cleaning on her own.

I worked for a while for a man named Mr. Rudolph, but he fired me. So I looked in the back of the building and saw there was a station and dryer that wasn't being used. I am going to work here, I thought.

"Mr. Rudolph," I asked, "How much for this station over here?"

I didn't have any customers at the time and he's thinking he'll get some easy money while I waste my time. "It's $600 a month," he replied. It was a long time ago and things were cheaper then.

"That's too much, but I'll pay you $100 a month."

He agreed with that so I started going out and meeting people and making friends. All my new friends start coming to me to do their hair and I start making money — enough money that Mr. Randolph started thinking he let me have the station for too little money.

One day he came to me and said, "Nida, I'm going to have to close your station.

"Why?"

"Because you're making too much money and I'm not making anything with it."

"Well we discussed it and agreed that I would only pay you $100. You can't go back on it now just because you're not happy anymore. We agreed on $100 so that's what I'm going to pay you."

"No. That's not going to work for me." "Remember, we had an agreement." "Yeah, but that doesn't count anymore."

"Well it counts for me," I said.

"Fine, you can stay at $100 for now, but not too long."

So, I kept working there, but after a while he started getting very worried because his son got very sick with bad asthma. One day, he was telling me about how sick his son was.

"Mr. Rudolph," I asked him. "What are you going to do for your son?"

"What do you mean? There's nothing I can do. The doctor says there's nothing he can do either."

"Well," I said, "there's something I can do. When I was a young girl in the Philippines, I was very sick with asthma. I almost died. But they cured me with traditional medicine. I know what they did and I can do it for your son."

"What did they do?" he asked.

"They caught these noisy little bugs that were in the houses in the Philippines. They go "eet, eet, eet!" First, they took two of them and roasted them until they're crispy. Then they ground them into a powder and put it in some water. They didn't tell me what they were doing at the time, they just told me to drink it and of course I did.

Soon after, I was all better and didn't have trouble breathing anymore."

"You're really going to feed my son bugs?"

"Hey, if it works, then he's better and if it doesn't he's no worse off than he is right now. But before I give it to him, you have to write down that it's not my fault if anything bad happens and that you won't sue me."

He agreed and told me I could try it. I didn't have to catch the bugs because over here in the United States I could just buy them. I made up the bug water just like they had done for me in the Philippines. When I told Sherman what I was doing, he ran away because he thought I'd kill the little boy and get put in jail! But in the end, it helped him and he lived. After that, Mr. Randolph and I worked together much better.

One of my neighbors in Klamath Falls was named Carol. She had red hair and only one leg. Her husband was named Connie, and every time he got paid, he would go to the local tavern and pay for everyone's beer. One day she came over to the house.

"Nida," she said. "Can I borrow some sugar?"

"Sure, Carol," I said. "But why do you need some sugar? Don't you have any?"

"It's Connie's payday, so he's over at the bar spending it all on buying drinks for everyone. I don't have enough money to buy food for the kids.'

"Go put on your ugliest clothes on you and your kids. We're going to go get him.

While she was doing that, I got dressed up real pretty in my best minidress, since Carol said that's what Connie liked. When we were ready to go, we all got in her car and drove to the bar. I told her and her daughters, Judy and Linda, to crouch down in the seats so nobody could see them, but to be ready to open the door when I come back out.

I went into the tavern and sat down near him. He was so drunk, he didn't recognize me, even though he's my neighbor.

"Hi," he said to me.

"Hi," I replied. "It's hot today. Wanna buy me a drink?

"Sure. What do you want?"

"A whiskey, half a glass."

He told the bartender to get my drink and I invited him to come outside with me. He happily followed me outside. As soon as we got out there, I signaled to Carol to open the back door. We walked over to the car, and he's so drunk it was easy to just shove him in the back seat. A quick push and we drove off with him in the back with the girls! When we got back to their house, I had her take his wallet and keys. Then we pushed him out of the car and onto the lawn. Then we left him there while we went to the grocery store where Sherman was working part-time. I told him that we're getting some food and then started roaming the aisles. We got a bunch of oats and milk, since the kids like oatmeal for breakfast. I told Sherman to pay for it all out of his next paycheck and then went back home with Carol. The next morning, Connie wakes up in the grass and is embarrassed, but doesn't remember anything. When Carol told me that he doesn't remember any of it, I told her that we'd keep doing the same thing every payday until he stops doing it. Luckily, though, he never did it again.

While we were in Klamath Falls, Sherman got the news that he would be serving at Benoit Air Force Base in Vietnam. By then I was expecting our youngest child. Sherman realized he might not survive the assignment in Vietnam so we agreed that if the baby was a boy, we would name him after his father. Sherman, Jr. was born 8 months before Sherman came home, safe at last.

One day when Sherman called home from Vietnam, he told me that I shouldn't work and stay home. I should go out and have a good time. Since he didn't specify what he was thinking, I decided that meant I should go dancing. I talked Carol into going with me to the Non-Commissioned Officers club to dance. When we got there, I told Carol that we could only drink Coke and only dance the boogie — no alcohol and no slow dancing — because our bodies belong to our husbands. We had a wonderful time and danced a lot. Some of the men offered to take us home, but I told them no we had a taxi. The next time Sherman called, he asked me what I'd been doing.

"I've been dancing," I said, happily.

"Why are you going dancing?"

"You told me to have a good time, so I went dancing!"

"I never told you to do that! I said to take the kids out to do things at the park and zoo!"

"Well, you never said that, so I had a good time!" And I really did!

One day, I saw one of the other military wives crying, so I asked her what was wrong. She explained that her husband was stationed in Okinawa and that he had sent her a letter saying that he'd fallen in love with another woman and wanted a divorce.

"Ok," I said, "I'll tell you what to do. First, you go and dress yourself and your kids in the ugliest clothes you have so you look really poor. Then we'll go speak to the commanding officer. We'll get this fixed."

So, we went together to talk to the CO. She was crying and looking terrible, like her husband hadn't been taking care of her even before she was abandoned. I explained the situation to the CO and told him that he needed to do something about it. He agreed and made a call to the CO in Okinawa, who agreed to transfer him back in two days. I thanked him for his help and took her home.

"Ok," I told her, "now we will get him back. What kind of girl does he like?"

The next two days we spent giving her a makeover. We bought her a cute mini-skirt, because she said he liked that style best. Then I did her hair and make-up for her so that she looked sexy and beautiful.

She was there at the airport when he arrived, looking so happy to see him. When he got off the airplane, she ran and jumped into his arms. He looked stunned and happy, too.

The next day, he came to see me at the shop and offered to pay for her make over.

"She told me you helped her," he said. "l want to thank you for making her look so amazing."

"l don't need paid for helping her," I said. "She is a lovely girl. Now that you know too, make sure you take good care of her and don't go cheating on her again." "l promise," he replied with a smile.

I may be a busybody, but I just can't stop helping people, especially a crying woman.

Chapter 3

Military Wife

One day, I got a letter from Sherman saying that he was going to be re-stationed straight from Vietnam to Robins AFB in Georgia and I needed to move there. There I am, with five kids and no driver's license yet and I didn't have enough money to pay for transportation. I asked the military, but they wouldn't let him come home to help move the family to Georgia. I didn't know what to do, especially since I hadn't gotten any money from Sherman for several months, so I hadn't been able to pay the rent or bills for quite a while. So, I called the police and told them I was robbed and they were threatening the kids and I so I wanted protection. It wasn't true, of course, but they didn't know that and sent some officers to watch us. The Red Cross gave us a little money for food, but I didn't want to go on welfare. I went to the military office and told them that it was a huge emergency and that I needed my husband home right away. I made such a fuss that the military bank gave me $18,000 in back pay, so I finally had money to pay my bills. They didn't give it to my husband, either, they gave it to me.

They also arranged for Sherman to fly to the West Coast and drive us all to Georgia.

Sherman was home for six months before he found out what I did. My friends were jealous that I got the military to help me like that. They said, "Nida, I'm pregnant and I can't get the military to let my husband come home for the birth." I would tell them it's all a technique. What I did was go to the military bank and say, "I'm pregnant and about to have a baby right now. I'm not leaving until you get the CO here to talk to me! I'll have the baby right here in the bank if you don't get him!"

People were there quickly and I ended up with the $18,000 back pay so I could pay the rent and buy some food and bikes for my kids. It's all how you do it. You can't just give up.

One year, we didn't have any food or any presents for Christmas. On Christmas day, there was a knock on the door. When I opened the door, there was a decorated Christmas tree and a box of food on the porch! I never did find out who brought it. The food they gave us included a turkey, but I didn't know how to cook it, so I went to the neighbor and asked her to cook it.

"If you'll cook it, you can give some to us and keep the rest," I told her. She was happy to do that since she didn't have any food either. She cooked it so beautifully that I remember it as the best food I ever ate.

While we were living in Georgia, we took a vacation to Florida to go to Disney World. Janet asked to bring a friend and I let her. We all had a great time together. Another time, we went to California to visit Disneyland and Hollywood. I even rode the ET ride where you ride on a bike in the air like one of the kids in the movie. It was fun. We also went to the beach a lot. We were always going places because Sherman knows that I love to go, go, go, so he would take me all over the place. Since he was stationed in so many states over the years, we were able to see most of the United States. It made me so happy to be going places all the time.

I worked at a few different shops while we lived in Georgia. At one of them, there was a big incident. One of my co-workers was named Karen. On her day off, one of her customers came in and asked for me to do her hair.

"No, I can't," I told her.

"Why don't you want to do my hair?"

"Because you're Karen's customer and I don't want to come between you and her. I'm not like that."

She got really mad and started yelling for my manager. When he came, she started yelling about how she's going to sue us because I won't do her hair. So, I called Sherman to come and help. He came and asked what's going on.

The woman started yelling at him, too. "I'm going to sue you, and your wife, and the shop because she won't do my hair!"

I said "Sherman, I'm not gonna do it. She's Karen's customer and I'm not gonna take that money from her."

The manager called the boss, who said that he was going to fire me, but I wasn't going to let that happen!

"Ma'am," I said to the woman, "Right is right. You think you're gonna sue me?

I'll sue you for doing that to me!"

Pretty soon the woman backed off and left. Then I quit working at that shop.

"I don't wanna work here no more," I told them. "Not when you treat your people that way when they're being honest." They tried to get me to stay, but I wouldn't. I was always coming and going anyway, because I was married to an Air Force Sergeant.

You gotta be honest all the time because karma will get you. One time while we were still in Georgia, we went to the officer's club. My friend had called to tell me that we were invited to a party and that it was going to be an exclusive event. Sherman would need a tuxedo and I would need a long dress. Sherman got me a lovely, white dress with rhinestones along the neckline and a deep dip in the back. I was young and it looked so good on me. I put my hair up high and put baby's breath all over my hair. Sherman was working with a dentist at the base hospital at the time. The day of the event, the doctor's wife asked Sherman, "Is it true that your wife is a beauty technician?"

"Yes, she is."

Now, she was the type of person who is racist and who thinks she is something special because she is married to a dentist. When she came to the shop, she asked for Mrs. Watson and since she knows Sherman, she assumes that I'm white, too. When I come in and she sees me, she looks surprised. I have to be very careful, though, because her husband is an officer and Sherman is only a sergeant.

When she sees me she says, "You? You're Mrs. Watson?"

I can immediately tell what kind of person she is, but I was careful to be polite.

So, I said, "Yes, ma'am, I am. What can I do for you?" "Can you do my hair the way I want it done?"

"Thank you, ma'am for saying it like that, but I don't even know what you're talking about. I'm just a lowly beauty technician and you are like a queen. I'd better have Joyce help you. She does hair very well."

"You're right," she replied. "l should probably have my hair done by someone who is my own kind."

"Joyce will take very good care of you. Let me go get her."

I took Joyce aside and asked her to lower the temperature on the hair dryer so it would take a long time to dry. We all did that from time to time when we're dealing with those kinds of people. She agreed to do it and, sure enough, that lady was sitting there for hours! At 4 o'clock, her husband calls to ask me if she's done yet because they need to get ready. He started to get a bit rude, but I told him that I'm not in the military so he can't just talk to me any way he wants. The party started at 5 o'clock, but at 5:30 her hair was still wet.

"When will this be done?"

"About 7:00," we told her. She got so angry she just pulled out the curlers and threw them onto the floor before stomping out. I thought that's what you get and Joyce was all excited and said "l did it, Nida! I did it!" That's how we took care of each other.

At the party, the dentist tried to talk to Sherman about what happened, but Sherman told him that they should just let the wives sort it out themselves. They stayed friends despite us.

At one point, Sherman was stationed in the Philippines for two years, so the kids and I went with him. We lived outside the base and had a lot of fun visiting family and fun places. It was the first time that Sherman and the kids got to meet my surviving family — my brother and sister. Plus their spouses and children. We had a great time!

When we'd only been there for four days, a stranger approached me and said.

"Are you Nida?"

"Yes," I replied.

"Do you remember the woman you were sold to as a child?"
"Yes. Her name is Ungert. Do you know where she lives?"

"Yes, I know where she lives. "Can you take me there?"

"Sure. Follow me.'

I took all the kids and Sherman with me to visit her. The last time I had seen her was when I'd left her house. At that time, my last words to her had been "someday you will die in my arms because of the horrible way you treated me."

What I didn't know when we went to visit her was that she really was dying, and she knew it. I made her sit down and I told her "1 forgive you for what you did and I want you to forgive me, too." My son held her hand while I held her in my arms as she died. It was a very special moment.

One day, as we were walking around town, the kids heard some music playing from down the street. The music was coming from the other side of a wall and I knew that there was a bar back there, but the kids didn't know that. They thought the music was coming from a carnival or something. They started pestering me, wanting to see where the music was coming from but I kept telling them no. Well, they didn't like that answer, so Janet and Chuck looked around and found a big can, which they put against the fence. They took turns climbing on the can and trying to peer over the fence. I made them get down and told them "If you ever try this again, I'm gonna hang you up!" Some people might think that sounds harsh, but you have to be strict with kids sometimes. I didn't want them to see something they shouldn't. There are some things that is not good for kids to see.

Two years later, we were back in the IJS and living at Chanute Air Force base in Rantoul, Illinois. I found work at a nearby beauty shop that was owned by a gay man named Gene. He was so nice to me and I got along with him very well. One day, the FBI raided the shop. What I hadn't known was that his boyfriend was involved with drugs. All I knew was that these FBI guys had burst in and were digging through everything — including my stuff at the station I rented from Gene.

"What are you doing?" I demanded. "That's my property!"

I was so mad that they were going through my things for something I didn't do.

"Sorry, ma'am, but we have to go through everything," they said.

Naturally, I backed off and went over to Gene's office to find out what was going on.

"Nida," he cried. "I swear I'm innocent! It was my boyfriend who was doing drugs. I'm gonna end up in jail! Everything here is yours, now. I'm gonna lose it anyway, so you might as well have it."

"Have you got any drugs anywhere else?"

"Yeah, at home under my bed in the pillow. I swear I didn't do anything!"

"I'll take care of this for you," I said.

I slipped out of the shop and rushed over to his house, which he shared with his mom. When she answered the door, I told her that Gene had sent me to fetch something for him from his bedroom, so she let me in the house. I rushed to his room and found all the drugs with the pillow, which I tossed out the window. The FBI came along soon after and told me to get out of his room, so I left. As soon as it was safe, I went around the house and grabbed the pillow and rushed to my car. As soon as I could, I got rid of it by throwing it out the window on my way back.

When I got back to the shop, Gene was still crying that he was gonna die and that it was all his boyfriend's fault. I told him what I had done for him and he was so happy.

"Nida," he exclaimed, "can I kiss you?"

"No, you can't kiss me! I let you off this time, but if you ever do this again I will call the cops on you!"

"I promise I won't!"

"Well, you better not because I'm serious about calling the cops. And you better get rid of that boyfriend before he gets you arrested next time."

I watched him like a hawk after that to make sure he stayed out of trouble, which he did. I'm stupid like that sometimes when I'm helping people. I just need to help people when I can.

Chapter 4

Building the Dream

Eventually, we were stationed at McChord AFB in Tacoma, Washington, which is south of Seattle. I soon had a job there working at a shop owned by a man named Dennis. He assumed that I knew how everything worked, but it turned out they did things very differently from the other salons I'd worked at. The other girls who worked there really didn't like me, maybe because I'm Filipino or something, and took advantage of the fact that I didn't know how I got paid. In all the other places I had worked, the way I got paid was different from here. They treated me terribly, like I was their maid. They made me fetch their coffee, sweep up the hair from haircuts, clean their stations, and wash their towels. I thought this must be normal for new beauty technicians at this place and that I'm getting paid by the hour, so I just did whatever I'm told. I worked hard and did everything they wanted me to. I was happy, thinking I was one of them. Two weeks later, when I got my first paycheck, I had was shocked. It was only $26! I thought to myself you work this hard and they only give you $26? That's not gonna happen!

I marched into Dennis's office and said, "Dennis, can I talk to you, please?" I showed him my paycheck. "Do you see this? Why did you pay me this low? I worked hard for your shop and did everything I was told to do!"

"Nida," he replied. "Put that thing down. I want to explain things to you." set it down and tried to calm myself a little while I listened to him.

"Let me explain," he said. "Yes, you worked hard, but you did not cut much hair.

You get paid for cutting hair, not for doing the other work."

"Do hair? I thought I was just gonna do work around the store and do the hair later when I was trained."

"That's not how it works. I thought you knew that."

"Well, I'm new to this way of doing things and I didn't know so the other girls used me."

I started thinking about what to do and when I came up with a plan, I thought to myself. Ha! You think you're gonna use me? You're all gonna get it!

"Dennis," I said. "Here's what I want you to do. Take my $26 dollars as a down payment. I want you to call a photographer to take some pictures and then put an ad in the newspaper for me. I'll pay you the rest later."

He agreed, so I got to work. First, I found two good-looking people to be my models — a man and a woman. Then I gave them both very nice, short haircuts. When the photographer came, I had him take a picture of the front and the back of both of them. Then I put an ad in the paper that showed all four pictures and had my name, the name of the shop, and the contact information. Once the ad came out, all day long the phone was ringing and people are dropping in and all everybody hears is "Nida, Nida, Nida, Nida!" I'm working as fast as I can and stay until 11 pm. My first paycheck was $26, but the second one was $4000!

Dennis called me into his office after that and said, "Nida, everyone has been complaining about you. They want to know why you're the only one working."

"Boss, you know how those other girls treated me. Now that I'm the one paying for your place, you better take care of the ones who were giving me a hard time. If you don't I'll go somewhere else and take all those customers with me. I can do it too. Every time a new customer came, I had them write down their name and number, so don't think I'm lying to you!"

"What do you want me to do, Nida?"

"You tell those other girls to take care of me — sweep the floor, make me coffee. All the things they made me do before. Make them do it for me now. I want them to know how it feels when you cheat people."

So, he did! He made those girls take care of me and told them they'd be fired if they didn't.

He was a good boss and I was happy working there, but I'm ambitious and I wanted to go out on my own because my family was finally in a position to settle down for a while. I looked around and found a cute little shop with two stations, which I quickly rented. To my surprise, I ended up with a partner as well.

The Japanese have always been my enemies since they attacked my country and killed my father and brothers. But there had been a Japanese girl, named Violet, working at Dennis's shop with me. I may think of them as my enemies, but that doesn't mean that I treat them badly. I was sure that she hated me because every time we worked together she would watch me. She didn't talk to me, just watched me all the time. But she didn't bother me, so I didn't bother her.

So I was very surprised when she showed up at my new shop. I thought uh-oh, why is she coming here? I figured it couldn't be anything good and so I started pumping myself up for a fight.

"What do you want?" I asked her.

"l want to work with you."

"Why would you wanna work with me?"

"Because I like you. I watch you and you are very nice. You make good money.

So I want to learn from you."

"l don't have time to do your books and all that stuff."

"Please."

"Well, I don't want an employee, but you could be my partner if you want. You can use the other station, but you have to keep your books and we'll split the money. You have your customers and I have mine. We won't tell each other what to do with the other person's customers. The money we just split in half. You wanna do that?" "Yes," she said. She was happy to work with me because she knows I'm honest. We got along well and soon customers were lining up. They would pay $15 a haircut.

Every day, I'd work hard until 5 o'clock, but then I would leave to go to the horse race track. Violet would stay behind and keep working, but I was out having fun. I only take $20 to gamble, making $2 bets each time. Usually I win, but sometimes I lose.

I just have fun because since it's only $20, so it doesn't matter if I lose it all. I knew that if

I took more than that I'd lose everything I have.

One day, I went back to the shop after gambling and Violet was still there, as usual.

"When you're done with that customer, can we talk?" I asked her.

When the customer was gone, I sat her down and said, "Violet, it's not fair the way we've been doing things. Every day, I leave at 5 o'clock, but you stay here and keep working. Those are your customers and your pay, not mine. When I leave at 5 o'clock, you keep the rest of the money for the rest of the day. I don't use people, so you keep what's yours."

So that's what we did from then on. Sherman asked me once why we never fought. I told him it's because we treated each other honestly and fairly.

One day, I asked her what the word "banzai" means. I had heard the Japanese soldiers yelling it when they were attacking the people in my village when I was little, but I didn't know what it meant and I had always been curious about it. She told me that the word means to kill.

After only two years working together, we had so many customers that we just didn't have enough time for all of them.

"Violet," I said to her one day, "I think it's time for us to separate. We have too many customers for such a small shop."

"You mean you want me to go back to Dennis's shop?"

"No, you're not going back to his place! You're a professional and you can have your own shop and get your own people working for you. I'll help you find a place." "I'm scared."

"There's no reason to be scared. You have lots of customers who will go with you to your new place."

So I helped her find a place of her own and get it all set up. When she left, she thanked me for helping her. Years later she was driving a Jaguar and playing golf. When I visited her, she took me out to eat. I was very happy for her. I'm never jealous because I like to help people. I'm happy because I like helping them succeed.

After helping Violet get set up in her own big shop, it felt weird being in my own tiny shop by myself. I didn't like it. I decided that I should get a nice big place of my own, so I started looking around for a bigger place for myself. Eventually, I found this nice, big building with big pillars in front. It looked like the White House. It was very nice and it was for rent.

I went to the real estate office that was in charge of renting it, but it was raining very hard that day and by the time I got inside their office, I was drenched. I walked up to the desk and told the receptionist that I wanted to rent that building.

"We only work with professionals," she said condescendingly.

I left, feeling very discouraged. But when I got back to my shop and started thinking about it, I thought I'm a professional. I have a degree and a license. How dare they! So I called the office and told them that I was coming back and they had better have their manager ready to talk to me.

When I arrived, I marched up to the receptionist desk and said, "You were rude to me earlier and I want to talk to your manager now. You said I'm not a professional, but I am and I want to rent a building for my hair salon."

She tried to ask if she could help me, but I said "No. You had your chance and you were rude. Now I expect the manager to help me."

They finally brought him to me since I wouldn't let anybody else help me. "Can i help you, ma'am?" he asked when he came into the lobby.

"Yes, thank you, sir," I said. "l came earlier today to ask about renting a place, but they wouldn't help me because they said I'm not a professional. But I am a professional and I can pay."

"I'm sorry that you had that experience, ma'am, and I will discuss this with them later. How can I help you right now?"

I told him which building I wanted to rent and offered to pay $800 as a down payment. I knew that my father-in-law, Jim Watson, would help me pay it, and he did. Soon, I was going to a top design company in Portland to have them do my floor plan. I told them that I wanted it to have twelve stations and picked out the flooring, mirrors, and lights and everything like that. Then I went to the beauty supply store and picked out the chairs and dryers. Everything I picked out was beautiful and top quality. Sherman and his co-worker built the custom counter and everything. When it was all done, it was lovely there!

Of course, all my old clients were happy to come to my beautiful new shop, but I had eleven empty seats to fill if I was going to pay all the bills! Where to find some hair stylists to work for me? Well, I looked around and saw a Macy's down the street. I knew they had a beauty salon in there, so I went to check it out. I let them do my hair and, while we were chatting, I figured out that maybe some of them weren't super happy about how they were treated there. So I invited them to have lunch with me at the Denny's across the street from my shop. It would be my treat. Well, who wants to say no to free food? They showed up and, while we were eating, I pointed to my shop.

"That's my new beauty shop," I said proudly. "It has the best of everything, but I need some good people to work with me and I like how you guys work. You should come over for a tour."

They agreed to a tour and, after they saw how nice and new my shop was, they all wanted to work there. They all had friends who wanted to work there too, so all the other seats were filled up in short order!

There were a lot of beauty shops in the area when I opened up. There were so many salons that most people told me that I'd fail because there was just too much competition, but I just wouldn't listen. I prided myself to always do better than my competition, and customers like that. I always told myself God gave you this brain so you can use it. Whenever I thought about what to do, the answer always came. I was always thinking about what I could do to make the shop succeed. I would ask God for help so that I would be able to help a lot of people.

One thing I did was send one of the stylists to Gerald Hair Design School in California to learn the top American styles and another one to school in Toronto, Canada to learn the top European hair styles. When they got back, I had them teach everyone else so that we're all up-to-date on the latest trends. I also put their names and certifications in the paper and in front of the station they worked at. I would send all the high flautin customers to those two because they were impressed with their credentials. I also made sure the two specialists were happy working at my shop so they wouldn't want to go work somewhere else. The shop was already really busy, but it became packed after that with all kinds of high-class people who would pay $80-90 for a haircut. I worked as hard as everyone else.

Sometimes, someone I knew who was not rich would come for a haircut. I didn't want to be rude and turn them away, but I also knew that the rich clients would be offended at having a regular person sitting next to them. So as soon as the normal person came in, I would wrap them in a cape before escorting them to their station. I did this so it would be impossible to see what they were wearing so they wouldn't be judged. Since I knew they couldn't afford my usual fees, I would only charge them about $30.

It was funny, because the first time I did a perm, it took me forever. My boss at the time would zip right through them like it was nothing, but I didn't know how to do it. So I asked him. He explained that the trick was to first, put a lot of hair in the curlers at once instead of small chunks and then second, get one started and then start another while the first was setting. By working on three at once, I could easily make lots of money since I was charging $85 each.

It's really funny, but even the way you speak can make rich people think you're one of them. I used big words when I'm talking to big, important people to let them know I'm in their class. You have to do that when you're in business. I used small words with my friends and family and talking for myself. One time, my friend invited me to go with her to a hotel to use their hot tub. It was a big, comfy one and there were some strangers there. They were all talking about all the fancy things they have and I felt like a no body next to them. I hoped they'd ignore me, but they started talking to me and asked what business I have. I told them I'm just an executive who just goes to work every day and then goes home to sleep. It's easy to bluff your way through situations like that. I figured that would shut them up, but then they asked me if I had any property. I told them I didn't want to talk about it because it was giving me problems.

I'm not like that by nature, but you do what you need to in order to survive with the rich.

I'm not the type of person who sits around crying or getting discouraged. I'm always looking for ways to do things and keep making things better. My shop was a great place to work. It was always busy and everyone working there always got along very well. I hated it when people said they worked for me, so I'd tell them that we work together so that we all can get rich. Everything we did was to make things better for all of us. I worked with them and as hard as them. They knew their place and I knew my place. I would tell my co-workers that they were also the boss, so they should handle any complaints on their own. I only stepped in if they really and truly couldn't take care of it by themselves. I always included them in everything I did because I meant it when I told them that I wouldn't make money without them. That's why they all loved me.

It was that desire to help them that prompted me to do a hair show. I arranged everything myself. I found some models, I picked out all the clothes, flowers, and jewelry, and I even ordered catered food for the event. Macy's allowed us to hold the event at their store because it showcased their clothes. The jewelry was leant by local jewelry shops. I rented a spotlight so everyone could see the front and back of the model's hair. One of my stylists was a gay guy and I got him to teach the models how to move correctly. Guests were told everything about what the model was wearing and what kind of haircut it was. When I gave my speech at the start of the show, I told everyone that my father-in-law, Jim Watson, was there and was responsible for the event being possible since he'd given me the money to start the shop. He was happy when everyone clapped for him. I also got to be one of the judges for the modeling and hair-dos. It was exhausting preparing for it, but the results were amazing!

We charged the guests $5 each to come to the show. I took all the money we made and told my stylists that it was going to be used for a fun recovery day. I had them close up the shop for the next day and to bring their families to the beach. We all stayed in the hotel for the night and caught crabs and ate them together. We all had so much fun together. That's why they all loved me and cried when I left. We did many of these shows over the years.

I worked hard for everything I had. I accomplished it all without having ever been to school the whole time I was growing up. I never got to go to elementary school, let alone high school or college. The only school I went to was to learn to be a beauty technician. Yet for all that, even people with college degrees would watch me to see how to be successful. Paris Beauty Supply even sent someone to find out what I was doing to be so successful. They said they wanted to pick my brain. I would just tell everyone to use common sense. That's not something you can learn in school. I would just think to myself Nida, what do you need to do to be the #1 beauty shop in Seattle? Then I would just go do it. That's why I started doing hair shows. Other places would charge $50 for guests to come see their hair and I'd go every time so I could see how to do a show better for myself. I always did things my way because it's the best way for me. I always wanted to make sure to do things high-class because when you do that, it's the high-class people who come. If you want to make lots of money, you need to cater to the rich ones. Our customers in Tacoma were mostly rich people, so I made sure to cater to them and keep them happy. I didn't care if they were rude or yelled at me, so long as they paid for their services. I didn't mix rich and poor customers and I did what I could to please the customers. I was always thinking of how to do things better and safer.

Chapter 5

Mothering

All the time that I was working hard in the beauty shops, I was also a mother. I had five children in the end. Janet, Charles (Chuck), Leja, Jason, and Sherman, Jr. I was always busy making money, but I also tried to be a good mother as well. Parents are very important because they're the ones who brought the child into this world. Even though I worked, I made sure that they wouldn't be left alone. First thing in the morning, I would cook breakfast before they went to school. Once they left, I would get dressed and go to work. I would work all day until around 3:00, when I knew it was time for them to get home from school. Then I'd make dinner so we could eat together as a family when my husband got home from work. As they got older, I could stay later at work, but I would always be sure to be there for them when they needed me.

It's so important to teach your kids responsibility. When they were little, they'd get home from school and immediately say, "Mom, can I go to my friend's house next door?

"Have you got homework?" I would ask.

"Yes."

"Of course you can go to your friend's house. But you need to do your responsibility first."

"Ok, but can I go now?"

"Honey, you heard what mom told you. Do your homework first. Then you can play."

"Ok, mom."

"Remember, you always need to do homework first because I always check with your teacher to see if you have homework."

When they turned sixteen, each of them was expected to go get a job as well. Homework and jobs taught them to be responsible people. Now they are all grown and are very successful people. They have all had great careers and did very well.

Of course, it wasn't always so easy. I got a friend to give Jason a chance by working at McDonald's. He was angry that I made him do it and didn't want to work for anyone. So he would stand at the grill and flip the hamburger so high it got stuck on the ceiling. Of course he got fired.

My friend said, "Nida, I am so sorry. I had to fire your son. All the hamburgers ended up on the ceiling!"

Jason came home and said, "Mom. You can take this job and shove it!"

So I took him to the recruiter's office and told him: "Sign!"

Then I had to sign too. Then I didn't worry about him any more. He stayed the full four years. He was never a problem after that. He got a good job and is respectful and does well.

The other thing I taught them is that it's important to keep yourself clean. I would always tell them to live so that they can wear white at their wedding. I would never tell them whom to love, but I expected them to be able to wear white when they get married. "Mom!" they'd exclaim when I'd tell them again. "You know I'm going to wear white. What you taught me did go in my brain, you know!"

All of my kids got married in white and only one of them got divorced. I'm so happy that I have such wonderful children! It's important to stay close to your family because they're the ones who will always be honest with you. I'm so proud of all my children and who they've become.

We really had some good times when they were growing up. We took lots of trips to fun places. One time, Sherman entered Leja in a beauty contest when she was three years old. He had to take her to all the events because I was too busy working. I did her hair, but my husband had to be the one to change her clothes! She was so cute up there on the platform. She almost won, but she didn't because the mother of the winner was one of the judges. Janet was also in a beauty contest in high school but didn't win because she didn't have enough money for all the things they had to buy. When the other girls bullied her, she slapped them! Karate lessons came in handy here.

One time, Janet asked to spend the night with a friend. She was sixteen, so I told her that she's old enough and she could go. While she was there, the police came. One of the policemen touched her butt and Janet did not like that so she jumped up on top of the police car and gave those two policemen a karate kick! She's just like me; she's mean when she gets angry.

There was another time when my neighbor gave me a pretty potted plant. I told Janet she should give it to her teacher, so she took it to school one day. When she came home after school, she asked me, "hey, mom, where did you get that plant?" "The neighbor gave it to me," I replied.

"Well, mom," she said. "The teacher was yelling at me because it was a marijuana plant!"

When Janet was a little older, she fell in love with a nice boy. One day she came to me and said, "Mom, I want to get married to my boyfriend, but we don't want to get married at home. We want to elope so it doesn't cost you and dad anything."

"I haven't met him yet. Is he a good boy?"

"Yes."

"Can you wear white?"

"Yes, mom."

"Ok, then that's good enough for me. You can do what will make you happy."

So she eloped with her boyfriend and moved to Ohio with him. She was there for quite awhile, and gave birth to our first grandchild there —a cute little boy. One day, I got a call from her. She was crying and said, "Mom, I can't take it here anymore. I can't get along with his mom." "Well, what do you want to do?"

"Can I come home?"

"Of course! You're my daughter and you can always come home."

"But I don't have enough money to come home."

"That's ok. I'll come get you."

"Thank you for always caring for me, mom."

So I fetched her home with her little boy and moved her home with us. I also gave her a job as a receptionist in my shop. I had space for two receptionists there, but I gave her the main spot because she's my daughter.

One day she came to me and said, "Mom, I miss my son's daddy. Can you please bring him here?"

"You know I've never met him."

"Yeah, but he's a good man, mom."

I trusted her because you have to trust your kids. "Yeah, you can bring him."

"You're gonna let him stay?"

"Yeah."

She hugged me tightly for that one. I bought him an airline ticket and a couple of days later he was here. There wasn't really enough room at the house for all of us, so I got them an apartment and leant them Sherman's car for six months. I found him a job doing vending machines. It was a good job that paid good money.

One day he told me that he wants to go into plastics, but it's a hard job to learn.

"Is it a good job?" I asked.

"Yeah."

"Then keep working hard at it until you like it and soon you'll get very good at it."

He learned everything he could about it because once he'd learned the hard stuff, everything else he needed to learn about it seemed easy. He applied at Boeing and they hired him right away because of what he knew. When you have a choice, always do the hard thing first.

I had a good friend named Ann. One day she asked me to go to Cancun with her. "Go home and pack your bag," she said. I knew Sherman would say "no" if I told him, so I decided not to tell him. I was about to pack my bag, then realized Ann and I were the same size. I'll just wear her clothes, I thought to myself. So I just jumped in her car without packing any bags!

When we got to the airport, she said, "where is your bag?"

"Right there," I said, pointing to her bag.

"What?"

It was too late to go back for my clothes, so we went without them.

We stayed at a 5-star hotel. We danced for hours, but only had one drink. Later, we flopped across our beds in exhaustion.

"Nida, close the blinds," she said. "The light is in my eyes."

"Close them yourself! Do you think I'm a servant or something? You rich bitch!"

I could say that to her because we teased each other a lot!

Another day we had a basket and went shopping and bought a lobster.

"What are you going to do with that?" Ann asked.

"Cook it! What you think I'm gonna do with it?"

There was a Mexican lady watching us. She looked poor and hungry, so I bought another and gave it to her.

"Gracias!" she said happily. It's good to be able to help others who need it.

Another night I said, "Let's go dancing!" For some reason, though, Ann didn't want to stay and dance. She was ready to go.

"Take your shoes off, then," I told her. I took them to the front desk and asked them to keep them safe for me.

"Nida, where are my shoes?"

"You're not getting them back 'till I'm ready to leave!"

We had so much fun!

There was another time I went to Mexico with a lawyer to see this tribe of tiny people who lived there. When we arrived, we stayed in the penthouse of the hotel. I could look out over the whole town from my window there. When I went down for breakfast, they gave me a giant load of bread and a papaya to eat. I thought that was just the perfect size meal for my breakfast, because who could eat more than that? But then they brought out the steak, the vegetables, the cactus, and the scrambled eggs. It was way too much for me to eat! When I told them that I couldn't eat it all, they thought that I didn't like the food. They thought I was being a picky eater. I told them that I did like it but that I just didn't have enough room for it all, but they still didn't believe me. It's their culture to feed guests a lot of food. In the end, I had them put my leftovers in a bag, which I threw in the trash. They weren't happy about that, either.

When Sherman retired from the Air Force, he decided we should move to Portland, Oregon because he'd gotten a job at the dental school there. He had graduated from there and would be helping students get admitted to the school. I wasn't too happy about moving because I owned four successful salons at the time. I sold them, though, and we moved away. My co-workers were so sad to see me go. They cried when I left. But it was time for our next grand adventure in life. Life keeps changing and takes us here and there. The only thing that stays the same is that you can see the fun and excitement in your life, no matter where you are.

Now my final big adventure in life is to share my story with others through this book and speaking to groups. I feel deeply indebted to my father for his love and wisdom when I was so young. My life has been spent trying to live up to his wishes for his, and my own, grandchildren and great-grandchildren, who he never got to see. I am also grateful to be an American. I am glad my father taught me the importance of helping others in spite of personal risk.

So, my final advice to you is to THINK! Use the brain God gave you to help yourself, your family, and others. Umunlad! [Darlene: That was supposed to translate to "Thrive!"] Love, Nida.

CPSIA information can be obtained
at www.ICGtesting.com
Printed in the USA
LVHW090449261020
669798LV00004B/20